GOOD THING

BY JESSICA GOLDBERG

★

★

DRAMATISTS
PLAY SERVICE
INC.

2

GOOD THING received its world premiere by Center Theatre Group/Mark Taper Forum (Gordon Davidson, Artistic Director/Producer) in Los Angeles, California, on May 23, 2001. It was directed by Neel Keller; the set design was by Jason Adams; the lighting design was by Rand Ryan; the sound design was by John Zalewski; the costume design was by Christal Weatherly; and the production stage manager was Victoria A. Gathe. The cast was as follows:

LIZ .... Megan Austin Oberle
DEAN .... Hamish Linklater
BOBBY .... John Cabrera
MARY .... Karina Logue
NANCY ROY .... Shannon Holt
JOHN ROY .... Francis Guinan

GOOD THING was subsequently presented by The New Group (Scott Elliott, Artistic Director; Andy Goldberg, Associate Artistic Director; Elizabeth Timperman, Producing Director; Jill Bowman, General Manager) at the Theater at St. Clement's Church in New York City on December 16 2001. It was directed by Jo Bonney; the set design was by Neil Patel; the lighting design was by James Vermeulen; the sound design was by Ken Travis; the costume design was by Mimi O'Donnell; and the production stage manager was Erika Timperman. The cast was follows:

LIZ .... Alicia Goranson
DEAN .... Hamish Linklater
BOBBY .... Chris Messina
MARY .... Cara Buono
NANCY ROY .... Betsy Aidem
JOHN ROY .... John Rothman

CHARACTERS

LIZ — 21, lost but street smart, cynical

DEAN — 23, proud young memeber of the American working class

BOBBY — 21, Dean's brother, a speed addict

MARY — 21, Dean's wife, eight months' pregnant, sweet, an ex-speed addict

NANCY ROY — mid-40s, inner-city high-school guidance counselor

JOHN ROY — mid-40s, guidance counselor, ex-hippie type, the kids love him

PLACE

Somewhere in upstate New York.

TIME

The present.

GOOD THING

ACT ONE

Scene 1

Anakonda Kaye Sports Store in the mall. John and Nancy Roy are buying sneakers.

NANCY. *(Exasperated.)* How about those?
JOHN. Too fancy?
NANCY. Maybe.
JOHN. These are simpler. I think I prefer simple. Maybe you should try them?
NANCY. I like the ones I've chosen.
JOHN. They just got so complicated, sneakers.
NANCY. Just pick, c'mon, we've been in here over an hour.
JOHN. I just don't understand all this mesh and color and what would you call this?
NANCY. I don't know.
JOHN. No really, what would you call it?
NANCY. I don't know.
JOHN. It's like a bubble, a colorful hard bubble.
NANCY. Oh god, it's a shock absorber, it's for basketball or running, whatever's rough on the knees, I don't know, do we always have to —
JOHN. My knees are bad.
NANCY. *(Trying to keep calm.)* Well then, get it, try it, I think the shock absorber would be great for you.
JOHN. I don't know, too young for me?
NANCY. Oh John see, this is it, the epitome of —

5

JOHN. Look, pipe down.

NANCY. Pipe down? I'll be in the car.

JOHN. Wait. Just wait one second. Have I tried these?

NANCY. Yes, god. I am going to cry, John.

JOHN. Look I'm sorry, just relax, okay?

NANCY. I am going to buy my sneakers.

JOHN. Look, all I want is a simple sneaker, a simple sneaker I can hike in, that's all.

NANCY. I am going to pay for these.

JOHN. I just don't know which ones to get, can't you understand that? *(Quiet.)*

NANCY. Maybe if I leave it will be easier for you.

JOHN. Yes.

NANCY. I'll be waiting in the car. Please don't make me wait all day.

JOHN. No, no, here, these — *(He grabs a pair of shoes he has tried on five times.)* These were good, right? *(She looks as though she might cry. Liz enters in an Anakonda Kaye outfit and visor, a Polaroid camera around her neck.)*

LIZ. Hi, can I help — oh Mr. Roy, hey! *(John looks blankly at her, she lifts her visor.)* It's me, Liz.

JOHN. Liz. This is my wife, Nancy.

LIZ. Hi.

NANCY. Hello.

LIZ. Gosh, it is so good to see you.

JOHN. You too, Liz was a ... a student, when did you graduate, Liz?

LIZ. Three years ago —

JOHN. Wow.

LIZ. This is my first time back since.

JOHN. Well great, how is ... college?

LIZ. Ithaca.

NANCY. Cornell?

LIZ. No, just Ithaca, but I dated someone from Cornell, Ithaca.

JOHN. Liz is one of my success stories.

NANCY. That's great.

LIZ. *(To Nancy.)* He's really an amazing guidance counselor.

JOHN. *(Humble.)*   NANCY.

Oh well —   So I hear.

LIZ. You don't have the slightest idea of how much of an effect

6

you have on us — me at any rate, do you?

JOHN. Well, well, I like to hope, but you know, that's nice, very nice …

NANCY. What's your major?

LIZ. Well, pre-med. It was.

JOHN. Oh wow, a doctor, how great, how great. Isn't that something? One of my kids is going to be a doctor.

NANCY. Mmmm …

LIZ. Well, I quit.

JOHN. What? Ithaca?

LIZ. No, no, it's good, really. Remember I sat in your office, I was seventeen and so confused. You said, "If you don't go you'll never know," you said: "Our power as human beings comes from our ability to make informed choices."

JOHN. Huh.

LIZ. *(Nods.)* And so I got to find out.

JOHN. Oh.

LIZ. Like I'm really gonna be a doctor, bullshit. *(Beat.)* I really have you to thank for that, Mr. Roy.

JOHN. Well, that, that's good to know, and I uh, really appreciate that. *(Liz nods.)* You know, funny thing with life, Liz, most of the time we've got everything we need, all the answers, right there inside us, we just don't trust ourselves.

LIZ. Yeah, totally, you're so right, so right. They should like make a little Mr. Roy doll you can carry around in your pocket for good advice.

JOHN. Hah! Wouldn't that be … pocket guidance counselors, they could really make some money —

LIZ. I think so —

JOHN	LIZ.
Yeah, huh —	Yeah.

NANCY. Well, we should pay.

JOHN. Oh yes. So I guess we'll be charging these today, going deeper into debt. *(Nancy and John laugh halfheartedly.)*

LIZ. Oh, I hate to do this but I'm like required. We have a special today, all the sneakers are twenty-five percent off if you sing "Take Me Out to the Ball Game," we take a Polaroid of you singing. I mean I take a Polaroid, see, we hang it on the wall.

(She points to the wall behind her full of Polaroids of smiling faces.)
I know it's pretty lame, but it's probably worth the humiliation for the discount. I mean I'd discount you anyway but my manager over there is like Hawkeye, so you wanna do it? *(Nancy shakes her head no, begins backing away from the counter toward the exit of the store.)*
JOHN. No, I don't think so, not today.
LIZ. No, god I can't get anyone to do it. All the other employees have everybody singing … What a loser — right? You could just sing for me, since you know me, out of sympathy. *(John and Nancy look at Liz, a bit thrown.)* You don't have to do it very loud or anything. *(John looks toward his wife; she smiles faintly.)*
NANCY. Go ahead.
JOHN. Okay, okay: *(Sings.)* Take me out to the ball game, take me out to the park, buy me some peanuts and fucking cracker jacks … *(John and Liz laugh; Liz points the Polaroid at him. Nancy watches her husband. She does not smile.)* I don't care if I never get back. 'Cause it's root, root, root, for the home team, if they don't win it's a shame, *(John pulls Nancy into the picture.)* One, two, three strikes you're out at the old ball game! *(Liz snaps the Polaroid … a FLASH of light! Blackout.)*

Scene 2

Later that afternoon … A small kitchen. Dirty pink linoleum. Bobby, twenty, skinny, pimples, jeans and a T-shirt (same one for a week), is rolling up some hamburger meat into patties. A small Sony boombox sits on the kitchen table, something like The Beastie Boys — old-school, maybe "(You Gotta) Fight, for Your Right (to Party)" … is on.* Bobby sings along. On the stove, a plate sits on a pot of boiling water. Bobby is cooking a speedy drug, his own concoction. Bobby works on the burgers; he sings quietly to himself.

---

* See Special Note on Songs and Recordings on copyright page.

BOBBY. You wake up late for school and you don't want to go, ner, ner, ner, nah ner nernah ner nerneer ner. *(From in the house, Mary bangs and calls:)*

MARY. Bobby? Bobbb-yeeee!!!!

BOBBY. WHAT, MARE?!?

MARY. TALK TO ME!

BOBBY. Uhmmmm ... *(Bobby checks the plate.)* OKAY, BUT ONLY FOR A MINUTE. *(Bobby turns down the stereo. Mary continues to shout from off, somewhere in the house.)*

MARY. I GOT A NEW ONE.

BOBBY. WHAT?

MARY. MEG!

BOBBY. OH GOSH, THAT'S A CUTE ONE!

MARY. YOUR TURN. *(Bobby stares at the plate.)*

BOBBY. LATER, MARY, I PROMISE!

MARY. BRING ME A GLASS OF MILK! *(Bobby looks at the plate, concerned.)*

BOBBY. OKAY!

MARY. AND THINK OF A NAME, A BOY NAME. *(Bobby pours a glass of milk.)*

BOBBY. DAVID!

MARY. OH! NICE! *(Bobby goes off with the glass. From off, we hear ...)* Don't leave, please!

BOBBY. I'm sorry, Mary, I'll be back soon. *(Bobby comes back into the kitchen. He turns the music up louder. Gets into the awesome lyrics. From off, Mary bangs on the wall, calls. Bobby goes to the plate and scrapes some of the stuff off the plate, snorts it. He puts a pan on the stove, pours oil, rages ... the oil shoots up into the air. He sings:)* You miss three classes and no homework, ner, ner, ner, nah ner, ner ner, your teacher preaches class like you're some kind of jerk. *(He throws the hamburgers into the pan. The hamburgers sizzle, sizzle.)* You got to fight, for your right, to PART-TEEEE!!! *(Crossfade ... The Roys' kitchen. Nancy is cooking dinner. John enters the kitchen with a box of stuff he is throwing out; amidst the junk is a roll of child's wallpaper, still in its packaging. Nancy tries not to look at the stuff in the box, but her eye wanders there from time to time, she can't help it.)*

JOHN. Gosh this feels great, cleaning out, we shoulda done this —

JOHN and NANCY. Five years ago.

NANCY. I said it.

JOHN. You did, you did. Wow, that smells great.

NANCY. I don't know, too much salt?

JOHN. There is no such thing as too much salt.

NANCY. That's why your cholesterol —

JOHN. My cholesterol — I'm gonna be biking, hiking ... dancing ...

NANCY. No dancing.

JOHN. C'mon, you love to dance.

NANCY. Oh yeah? Since when?

JOHN. Since ... *(Takes out a photo from his pocket.)*

NANCY. Oh god, put that away.

JOHN. Why? It's gorgeous.

NANCY. It's, it's horrific, okay, let me see it, let me see it ... *(Looks at it quickly.)* Ewwww! Awful! Put it away, I never want to see that again. Where did you find that anyway?

JOHN. Attic.

NANCY. Well, it can stay there. *(John puts it back in his pocket.)*

JOHN. I'm keeping it right here, next to my heart.

NANCY. I thought it felt great, cleaning out.

JOHN. Yes, but not this, why would you want —

NANCY. Because it's old, the past, we're supposed to concentrate on now, the future —

JOHN. Yes, now, the future, but I'm not gonna throw away something that's beautiful.

NANCY. I just, I just don't always want to be looking back, you know? You love to look back.

JOHN. I do not love to look back.

NANCY. Sure you do.

JOHN. When?

NANCY. All the time you look back.

JOHN. On what?

NANCY. Photos, memories, ruminate, conversations —

JOHN. You're wrong.

NANCY. I just want —

JOHN. I don't do that, I am committed to the present.

NANCY. I just want, to be now.

JOHN. We are. You're so crazy. You were so beautiful.

NANCY. Were?

JOHN. Are. Are. I think you're the most beautiful woman in the world ... And the best goddamn cook in upstate New York!

NANCY. Set the table, John. *(Crossfade to ... Bobby lies on the kitchen floor. Dean stands above him, staring down at him. Dean is twenty-three. He wears work boots, jeans, he looks tired and dirty from a long day of construction.)*

DEAN. Bobby. Bob. *(He kicks Bobby lightly with his boot.)* Time to get up.

BOBBY. Oh hey Dean.

DEAN. "Hey Dean?"

BOBBY. How was work?

DEAN. The burgers Bobby?

BOBBY. Oh no, did they...? *(Dean nods.)* Oh shit, I'm sorry man, I don't know how it happened?

DEAN. Want me to tell you?

BOBBY. *(Shrugs, goes to speak.)* Well probably because —

DEAN. You're a crank-head.

BOBBY. Yeah. *(Dean sighs, goes to the refrigerator for a beer.)*

DEAN. Just a guinea pig, nothin' but a whore, Bobby. Whore to the system. Every time you take a snort, take a hit, you're just lickin' their balls.

BOBBY. You're right Dean. I know. It just feels good.

DEAN. That is exactly what they want you to think. They want people like us hooked, you see, Bobby. I'll tell you why too, 'cause we're smart and we haven't been to college and that makes us dangerous. That makes us —

BOBBY and DEAN. Very threatening.

DEAN. So they hook you and you're gone, no more threat.

BOBBY. Their loss though, huh? *(Bobby gives Dean a big, proud smile; Dean smirks, pleased in spite of himself, swats Bobby playfully.)*

DEAN. Yeah. Loser. *(They play-wrestle until they are on the floor. Suddenly Dean gets serious.)* How's she been today?

BOBBY. Fine.

DEAN. You let her out of the room?

BOBBY. No.

DEAN. *(Nods.)* I'm starvin', Bobby. *(Bobby sits up.)*

BOBBY. Hey Dean, how'm I a whore if I'm not gettin' any?

11

DEAN. What?

BOBBY. You said I was a whore. How'm I a whore if I can't get no peach?

DEAN. 'Cause you call it peach, asshole, and you snort that crap.

BOBBY. Yeah, but I make my own crap.

DEAN. Hey, if you want to be a casualty that's your choice.

BOBBY. What you don't get is how I'm using them.

DEAN. How?

BOBBY. I just am. I know I am. I'm breaking the rules and getting away with it.

DEAN. My stomach's growling like this was a third-world country. You wasted good meat, Bobby —

DEAN. *(From off ...)*	MARY. *(From off ...)*
That was good meat. I got it at Arty's, not the G.U.,	Dean? Dean?
Arty's, it probably cost four bucks a pound you got no responsibility, no understanding of what's got value —	Ya back? Dean?

BOBBY. She's calling you.

DEAN. Yeah. You talk to her today?

BOBBY. For a minute.

DEAN. What'd she say?

BOBBY. She said to come get her when you got home.

DEAN. Oh. *(Dean moves to the sink, begins to do the dishes.)*

BOBBY. Oh, let me do 'em.

DEAN. I got it —

BOBBY. No, I wanna, I wanna, let me. *(Bobby takes over at the sink; Dean takes his beer to the table, sits, spaces out.)* I like doing dishes, I like the feeling of warm water on my hands, it's very relaxing ... *(Bobby trails off, washes dishes, Dean relaxes, drinks his beer. Crossfade: the Roys' kitchen ... The Roys sit at the kitchen table eating dinner. Nancy notices John lost in thought, gives him a look ...)*

JOHN. Down, you were right, down.

NANCY. What?

JOHN. I was wrong, you were right, it will be cold. In Maine.

NANCY. Sleeping bags?

JOHN. Yeah.

NANCY. Oh.

JOHN. What?

NANCY. No, I just, I just thought we finished that conversation five hours ago.

JOHN. Well, I was thinking when I was cleaning out, it's time to spend some money on us.

NANCY. Sure.

JOHN. It's not like we have college tuitions or —

NANCY. Okay.

JOHN. You only live once, right? *(Nancy nods. Beat.)*

NANCY. There's something else.

JOHN. What?

NANCY. Something else you're thinking about —

JOHN. What?

NANCY. I don't know, I'm asking you. It could be anything, like the sleeping bags, something from hours, days, years ago.

JOHN. I was thinking ... about the girl, my student, from the sports store.

NANCY. Of course you were. *(Jokes.)* Did you sleep with her?

JOHN. *(Frustrated, shakes his head.)* What?

NANCY. No, I'm ... I'm sorry, what?

JOHN. I am not — *(Cuts himself off.)*

NANCY. I'm sorry, what were you going to say? What? I'm sorry. What were you going to say about her?

JOHN. Just that, her, dropping out, in her junior year, I don't know, makes me feel like ... useless, at my job. That's all.

NANCY. It's not your fault.

JOHN. No, I know. I know.

NANCY. Our influence is ... we can only do so much.

JOHN. Sure, yes, I know. But still, what was I talking about? "We have all the answers ... we just don't trust ourselves," god, I sound like ... *(He shudders.)*

NANCY. I do the same thing, get carried away sometimes. You told her what she needed to hear, it was very nice of you.

JOHN. I guess. I guess. The truth is, I didn't even remember her, not really, not for a few seconds.

NANCY. Well, she sure remembered you, that's what matters.

JOHN. How can we ... if we don't even remember them?

NANCY. There's so many.

JOHN. Yes. *(Beat.)* I am just so excited about Maine. Let's go out.

NANCY. We were just out.

JOHN. C'mon, we'll go pick up those sleeping bags, see a movie, we haven't seen a movie in …

NANCY. … Yeah? *(John nods a big yes.)* You don't mind missing your meeting?

JOHN. Oh.

NANCY. You forgot.

JOHN. Shit.

NANCY. Don't worry about it, it's fine.

JOHN. No, no, I can miss it — I'll find a meeting in Maine.

NANCY. On our vacation? Just go tonight, it's fine, I have so much to do anyway. *(Beat.)*

JOHN. What about the sleeping bags?

NANCY. We can order them on-line, the glory of technology, and that way you won't end up singing to any more of your ex-students, ha-ha. *(Beat.)* I'll get the catalog. *(Crossfade … In Dean's kitchen, Bobby, still doing dishes, remembers something.)*

BOBBY. Oh man, I forgot to tell you! Dean? Dean?

DEAN. Yeah?

BOBBY. Speaking of good meat.

DEAN. Yeah?

BOBBY. Guess who called?

DEAN. Who?

BOBBY. Liz.

DEAN. Liz? No way?

BOBBY. Yuhp.

DEAN. She called?

BOBBY. Yuhp.

DEAN. Here?

BOBBY. Yuhp.

DEAN. Liz? Liz?

BOBBY. Yeah.

DEAN. For me? *(Bobby nods enthusiastically.)* What'd she say?

BOBBY. She's gonna have a beer at The Joyous Lake later, you should come by.

DEAN. Tonight?

BOBBY. Eight o'clock.

DEAN. No way.

BOBBY. Yeah.

DEAN. She back? I mean for good, or she just visitin'?

BOBBY. I don't know.

DEAN. You don't know nothin', Bobby. And you just get stupid-er every day.

BOBBY. Stupid's good. Stupid's nice.

DEAN. Liz, man.

BOBBY. Peach.

DEAN. Yeah, she was.

BOBBY. Small, tight, nice ...

DEAN. Pick her up, put her on your cock, walk around the room with her. *(They laugh. From off ...)*

MARY. DEAN!!!! Dean! You home? Let me out!!! *(Dean looks off, looks down. Bobby gets up and moves to the table; he begins to scrape the rest of the concoction together on the plate.)*

BOBBY. So you gonna go to The Joyous Lake?

DEAN. Nah, wouldn't be right.

BOBBY. Yeah.

DEAN. Wouldn't be wrong though.

BOBBY. Sure.

DEAN. I'd be interested to see how she's doing, we were good friends, that's all it would be, like seeing a good ol' friend.

BOBBY. Sure.

DEAN. Plus you can't let marriage interfere with your personal freedom, that's what gets things sticky, all these people walking around like "I'm married I can't talk to you," causes resentment. Remember how Mom used to bag on Dad every time he went out?

BOBBY. He was fucking around. *(Dean is thoughtful. From off ... banging ...)*

MARY. Let me out! DEAN!!! Let me out!!!

DEAN. We better let her out.

BOBBY. Yeah.

DEAN. Will you? *(More banging ...)*

BOBBY. Okay. *(Bobby goes. Dean gets another beer, sits at the table. Bobby comes back in the room; Mary, extremely pregnant, follows behind him.)*

MARY. I was callin' you, Dean.

15

DEAN. Hey, Mary.

MARY. Didn't you hear? I called your name like twenty-six times.

DEAN. I didn't hear.

MARY. Did you make dinner, Bobby?

BOBBY. I burnt the burgers.

MARY. That's because you were, you know, right? You were, right? That's why they get burnt, because when you do that you space out, you space out and your body just tingles, but it's bad for you. Right, Dean?

DEAN. Yeah.

MARY. Dean cares about me and our baby. *(Mary sits on Dean's lap. He looks tiny beneath her.)* How was your day?

DEAN. Good. *(She looks at him eagerly, waiting for him to continue.)* We put the windows in the house today.

MARY. Wood or vinyl casing?

	BOBBY.
DEAN. Wood.	*(Begins to sing absent-mindedly to himself, quiet.)* Our house in the middle of the street, our house where the
MARY. No way.	*(Stops, thinks.)* used to meet. Our house, ba de dumpy dumpy dum … *(Etc.)*

DEAN. Well they've got the money, hey —

MARY. Would you? If you had the money?

DEAN. I don't know, it's pretty extravagant — I'd probably remain practical, go with the vinyl.

MARY. Spend the extra on some really nice interior trim.

DEAN. Wrap the windows in wood —

MARY. Between the two of us we wouldn't have to pay for labor, and I could do all the painting. *(Dean takes her hand lovingly.)*

DEAN. Yeah. *(Beat.)*

MARY. I had quite a day myself.

DEAN. Oh yeah?

MARY. Got through the Caverns —

DEAN. No way —

MARY. I'll show you later, Double O is ready to take on Trevlyn in the Cradle, beat the game!

DEAN. Impressive.

MARY. Tell me about it, my thumb is totally sore. Not to mention I'm almost done with the baby's afghan, which is good so I can get started on your winter hats and gloves.

BOBBY. I want green.

MARY. Yeah, Bobby, you tell me like every day you want green — Am I hurting you, Dean?

DEAN. No.

MARY. You keep gettin' smaller and smaller. I get bigger and bigger and you get smaller and smaller. That's your fault, Bobby, how you gonna feel if he gets so skinny I sit on his lap one day and squash him?

BOBBY. Stupid.

MARY. Yeah, stupid. C'mon, think. *(They laugh, it fizzles, quiet.)* So what'd you do today, Bobby?

BOBBY. Not much.

MARY. You did some, right?

BOBBY. What, Mary?

MARY. You know.

DEAN. I swear to god, I'll call your dad. *(Mary looks stricken with fear.)*

MARY. Don't do that. *(Changes her tone to happy.)* It's gonna come out soon, Dean. Any day now, it's gonna come out.

DEAN. Really? *(Mary gets off of Dean's lap, moves to the fridge, the cabinets.)*

MARY. Things'll be better when it comes out. I got a feeling, things'll be better. More normal. It's just got me tired all the time so I can't cook. I used to keep things going, I used to have energy, things used to be fun. Remember, Dean? We had fun, we kissed, we went to the movies, I was doing okay, right? Sometimes I didn't even at all, right? It's funny what being preggers does to you. Makes you smarter somehow. Makes the reality that much more clear, makes everything more clear, like having this thing in your stomach, was like gettin' new glasses, ones that work, only everything is much darker, seen for what it is.

BOBBY. You talk some cool shit, Mary.

MARY. Thanks, Bob. Dean? Dean?

DEAN. Yeah?

17

MARY. You think things will be better?

DEAN. Sure, of course they will. *(Dean and Mary smile at each other.)*

MARY. Me and Bobby named the baby before today.

DEAN. When?

MARY. While you were working.

DEAN. Thought she didn't talk to you today.

BOBBY. We just talk through the wall, Dean.

DEAN. What'd you name my kid?

BOBBY. We was just kidding around with names, joking.

MARY. Laughing. We laughed. Bobby makes me laugh. That's good. I need to laugh. My mom says that's what got her through, laughing and laughing.

DEAN. So what'd you name it?

MARY. We named it David and Meg.

DEAN. I hate Meg.

MARY. What's wrong with Meg?

DEAN. It's a pug nose girl name.

MARY. Pug nose girl name. You don't have a pug nose, I don't, so how's it gonna have a pug nose even if it's named Meg, Dean?

DEAN. I don't know. *(Beat.)* Shit, I'm starved —

MARY. Let's order Chinese, I could go with you to pick it up, I could use a drive.

DEAN. Well, I was thinking, something different, maybe I'd go out.

MARY. Where?

DEAN. I dunno.

MARY. Pick me up somethin'.

DEAN. Okay. What do you want?

MARY. Bring me a present.

DEAN. Okay.

MARY. How long you gonna be?

DEAN. Uhmmmm …

BOBBY. You goin' to The Joyous Lake?

DEAN. I'm gonna go see Liz over at the Lake and get somethin' to eat. She's back in town.

MARY. Oh.

DEAN. You wanna come?

MARY. Me?

DEAN. Yeah.

MARY. No.

DEAN. Bobby?

BOBBY. Nah.

MARY. You're going to see Liz? What is she, like back?

DEAN. Look, we were friends, me and Liz, and she's visitin' I guess, and I never get out of the house anymore. *(Mary rolls her eyes at him, humphs.)* Look, Mary, I didn't have to tell you who I was going to meet. If it was anything deceptive — like I coulda lied. Right, Mary? Right?

MARY. Remember that time in Cumbies that guy told me I had nice legs, he was drooling, and you smeared a box of doughnuts on his head? Remember? Remember, Dean?

DEAN. *(Smiles.)* Yeah.

BOBBY. That was a very stressful time, there were a lot of bills left from Mom gettin' sick.

MARY. Your heart, Dean, is soooo beautiful. *(Mary approaches Dean, goes to kiss him, her stomach brushes against him; clearly, he is terrified of her pregnancy. Mary senses this and backs up, covering:)* Baby's gonna have your heart, Dean. *(Dean nods.)*

DEAN. Let me get you something to eat, Mary beautiful, whad-d'ya wanna eat?

MARY. I wanna eat you, Dean, alive. *(Beat.)* Just a joke! You're all lookin' at me like I was a vampire. *(Bobby laughs.)*

BOBBY. That's funny, Mary.

MARY. Thanks, Bob.

DEAN. So I'll just have a quick one, bring back some food.

MARY. Yeah.

DEAN. Anything, Bobby?

BOBBY. Nah. *(Dean leaves.)*

MARY. It's just that he told me, no he didn't, but in his eyes, shit wasn't gonna be like this ya know? He made me feel so much better than I felt at home, ya know?

BOBBY. Yeah.

MARY. He didn't say it'd be different, but in his eyes, you know, there was something, like, like good, like protective. "We are the heart and soul of America." And his hands, big, and you ever feel them? Like wood, not sanded wood, wood with splinters, like a boxer. When the lights were out and his hands were movin' over

19

my skin I used to pretend that I was with this champ, you know? That got me crazy, made me feel so ...

BOBBY. Mary?

MARY. Yeah?

BOBBY. I got to lock you back in the room now.

MARY. You gonna get, you know?

BOBBY. Got to.

MARY. Lemme stay here, I swear I won't do it, it's been eight months.

BOBBY. Can't do that.

MARY. He went to go hang with Liz, that kills me —

BOBBY. He'll kill me, that's what'll kill.

MARY. I don't feel like bein' alone.

BOBBY. Mary?

MARY. Please, I promise to be good. I swear I won't do it, it's been eight months.

BOBBY. Can't do that.

MARY. Please, I swear, it's just if I go back in there I might kill myself, I'll just go crazy imagining he's with her and all.

BOBBY. I know but —

MARY. C'mon, I'll keep you company, we could play cards, we could play video games. It'll be fun, don't you miss havin' someone to talk to?

BOBBY. Yeah but —

MARY. I have no desire even, I'm over it, and I'm gonna have this baby any day now, and fuckin' Dean leavin' me like that, it's not right. I promise I won't tell him.

BOBBY. I, I ...

MARY. You're like my best friend, Bob, my only friend. Sometimes I wish I'd married you instead of him, sometimes, you ever wish that?

BOBBY. Little.

MARY. Yeah. We'll keep each other company.

BOBBY. You won't tell?

MARY. No. Shhhh ... *(Mary holds her finger to her lips.)*

Scene 3

Dean sits, drinking, at a small wooden table at The Joyous Lake. Liz has just arrived. She stands at the table.

LIZ. Dean.

DEAN. Bobby said eight o'clock, it's nine, thought you weren't gonna show.

LIZ. Had to wait for Mom to get the car home.

DEAN. Can't believe she still has a license.

LIZ. Oh, she doesn't. *(They exchange a look, a small smile of recognition.)*

DEAN. One sec. *(Dean leaves to go to the bar. Liz sits. Dean returns with four more drinks, puts them on the table.)*

LIZ. Four?

DEAN. Gets busy, hate waitin' ... still avoiding "the fate of your genes"?

LIZ. Good memory. *(Dean taps his forehead.)* I can't believe it's you.

DEAN. Yeah, Dean three years older, three thousand beers fatter. *(Dean pats a small beer belly.)*

LIZ. Please, don't even.

DEAN. Nah, you look good, college girl. *(Liz pshaw's him, rolls her eyes.)* Really. What's this thing you're wearing?

LIZ. This?

DEAN. Yeah?

LIZ. It's a tube top, stupid.

DEAN. Isn't that like a seventies thing?

LIZ. They're hip now.

DEAN. Ahhh, you're hip, hip, hip.

LIZ. Yuhp.

DEAN. Too hip for me, huh? Too hip.

LIZ. Maybe. Are you drunk?

DEAN. No, this is just my personality.

LIZ. I forgot.

DEAN. What?

LIZ. How obnoxious you can be. *(They exchange a smile.)* How are you?

DEAN. Great. *(She nods.)* So ah, you just poppin' through town? Decided to slum it with your ol' pal Dean?

LIZ. No.

DEAN. No?

LIZ. I'm moving, moved back, here, the other day. *(Beat.)*

DEAN. You did? *(Liz nods.)* What about college?

LIZ. What about it?

DEAN. You moved back here? *(Liz nods, smiles.)* For good? *(Liz shrugs her shoulders, like: I don't know.)* With your mom?

LIZ. For now.

DEAN. Then?

LIZ. Then ... I want to explain some things. I've learned a lot since I left ... at the time, I was afraid to tell you, you know, about school, leaving ... I have so many regrets about the way I ... you know?

DEAN. Regrets are the surest waste of time.

LIZ. Oh, well then, I guess I'll just not have them.

DEAN. Can't go through life: I wish I had said this or that to ... before they died or whatever ... could drive a man crazy.

LIZ. Well, yeah, not in that circumstance, but if there's still something you could do to change things, then maybe regrets are like a way of motivating you?

DEAN. I guess. *(They smile at each other, enjoy each other.)*

LIZ. You look good.

DEAN. Yeah?

LIZ. You do. You're gonna get better and better looking, you're one of those guys.

DEAN. That's cool.

LIZ. Still breakin' lots of hearts?

DEAN. Hey, I never hurt anybody.

LIZ. Yeah.

DEAN. Who wasn't already hurt. *(She smirks.)* Nah, really, it's all in the past, I'm a married man now.

LIZ. Yeah right.

DEAN. No, really, it does that to you, getting married, starting a family. No time to fuck around —

LIZ. What?

DEAN. What?

LIZ. Are you really? Who? Who are you married to?

DEAN. Ahuh, you don't — ?

LIZ. No, do I know her?

DEAN. Uhm, yeah.

LIZ. Who?

DEAN. *(Mumbles.)* Mary.

LIZ. Who?

DEAN. Mary, Mary Beck —

LIZ. Mary?!?

DEAN. What?

LIZ. No, I didn't.

DEAN. Keep your college attitude, Liz —

LIZ. No, I wasn't —

DEAN. Mary is a pretty amazing person, she changed a lot since you knew her —

LIZ. No, I'm sure, I mean we always liked Mary sort of.

DEAN. I see you haven't changed at all —

LIZ. I just didn't think you and her, no, I'm just surprised.

DEAN. You still think you're so much better —

LIZ. No, no I don't, I just —

DEAN. Of course you do, Liz, c'mon —

LIZ. I didn't mean to hurt you —

DEAN. Hurt me? Fuck you. *(Liz stands, on the verge of tears.)* What? Where are you going?

LIZ. I have to —

DEAN. I haven't seen you in three years and you're leaving —

LIZ. This is a nightmare.

DEAN. Wait. Just wait.

LIZ. No.

DEAN. C'mon. Sit. Okay? Sit down, I'm sorry,

LIZ. I'm sorry.

DEAN. We'll start over, okay? Okay? *(Liz looks at him, trying to decide whether or not to sit.)*

LIZ. Dean?

DEAN. We're starting over.

LIZ. Okay. *(She sits, beat.)* Wow, you, you have a baby?

DEAN. Having ... having.

LIZ. Congratulations.

DEAN. See, we're both doing what we always wanted to do with our lives. They were just different. We had different ideas, wanted different things, and we've got to respect that, about each other, those things, if we're gonna be friends I mean.

LIZ. Oh, I loved your ideas ... loved them so much, but then before, I'd never been ... I needed to see what else there was. Forget it. I don't know what I'm saying, we're starting over, screw it. Cheers! *(Liz picks up her drink, begins to down it; Dean watches her, somewhat amazed, as the whole drink slides down her throat. She puts the empty glass on the table.)*

DEAN. I see you learned some valuable skills out there at Ithaca. *(Liz picks up another drink, raises it to him.)*

LIZ. Well, I wish you the best.

DEAN. Yeah, you too. *(She smiles.)*

LIZ. I'm sorry I never said good-bye. Did you ever think about me?

DEAN. Sure.

LIZ. You did? *(Dean nods, yes.)* What? What did you think?

DEAN. Oh, one very important question always lingered in my mind.

LIZ. What?

DEAN. I wondered, did Liz lose it?

LIZ. My mind?

DEAN. Your cherry.

LIZ. You would.

DEAN. Did you?

LIZ. I thought about you.

DEAN. Did you lose it?

LIZ. None of your business, c'mon.

DEAN. I want to know, it's important to me.

LIZ. Why is it so important? Fine, yes, what's the big deal? *(Dean nods, taking it in.)*

DEAN. Didn't want to sleep with me, right? You were waiting for someone better, right?

LIZ. That's right.

DEAN. Was he?

LIZ. They?

DEAN. Hah, my loss.

LIZ. I guess so.

DEAN. Wow, higher education, keggers and one-night stands.

LIZ. *(Bitter.)* You don't know the half of it. *(An awkward beat.)*

DEAN. I'm gonna get another drink, want one? *(Liz shakes her head no.)* Aw, c'mon, we're getting all confessional, let's not stop now.

LIZ. I got her car. Mom's.

DEAN. I'll make sure you get home safe.

LIZ. I'm really trying not to …

DEAN. Relax, you're with a married man.

LIZ. All right, just one. *(Dean leaves to go to the bar; Liz watches after him. Liz takes the moment alone, to process the information — Dean is married. She looks around the bar, this place she remembers well, this place she has returned to, takes that all in. Dean returns with four more drinks.)* I said one.

DEAN. If you can't do it, I'll take care of it. *(She smiles.)*

LIZ. I had such a laugh, I was cleaning my room the other day, found this letter you wrote me. *(She pulls out a tattered letter, waves it in front of him.)* Remember this? *(Dean shakes his head no, even though he remembers. Liz begins to read the letter.)* Dear Liz, Truth as I see it aided by the all mind-expanding mushrooms. There is a desire on the part of the American establishment to change or ignore people like us, we must fight that attitude. They want us to "upgrade," they say: "This is America, the golden land of opportunity, get on board the ship, climb the ladder, son." What if we don't want to climb their stinkin' ladder? What if we love who we are? 'Cause they don't want us, they want upgraded us. They want them. It's bullshit! The spirit of the American people lies with us, if they succeed in their mission, the spirit of those of us born into Bruce's USA will be finished. Because we are beautiful, Liz, we are goddamn beautiful. All the times I get so down, feel sorry for myself, like why my mom? Why is my life so fucking hard? Now I know there's a reason and if we just wait we'll find out what it's all about. If we just push through and wait, then we'll know. *(Liz looks up at Dean, smiles; he smiles back at her, his face slightly red with embarrassment, but he holds on to his pride. Liz looks back at the letter. Her voice almost cracks.)* Care to wait with me? Love, Dean. *(Liz carefully folds the letter. They sit there quietly.)*

25

DEAN. *(Without anger.)* Funny huh. Good laugh. One man's dream is another man's nightmare.

LIZ. … Ginsberg?

DEAN. I don't know, thought it was just Dean.

LIZ. At my window sad and lonely, oft times do I think of thee, Sad and lonely and I wonder, do you ever think of me?

DEAN. Ughhh, Emily Dickinson?

LIZ. *(Shrugs.)* Woodie Guthrie. *(Dean: duh. They laugh, connect …)*

Scene 4

Split scenes: Bobby and Mary in the kitchen. Mary watches Bobby. Bobby rages around the kitchen.

BOBBY. Up for five days, five. No sleep, nada motherfucker, hairy prick. Didn't change our clothes, walking through the halls of Onteora, where's your hall pass? The bitch didn't even ask we musta been looking so bugged, man, remember? Chug cock, fucked up right? I was walkin' through the hall day number five, was gonna bust right out of my head, bust, thinkin', please ask me for my hall pass. Please, slow me down, ask me for my goddamn fucking hall pass. Please, right? Till the stuff was all gone, then I slept for a week, how many days you make it?

MARY. Three.

BOBBY. Three, right. Chug cock, hah, that is the funniest thing chug cock, you used to say that, obnoxious bitch, hairy prick, huh. See nows I know why you and Dean got together, and not me an' you, nows I know 'cause my thoughts are crystal clear now, my thoughts are pure, my thoughts are like water, I can see 'em, they make sense, I can hold 'em in my mouth, do you understand —

MARY. Tell me —

BOBBY. *(Running right over her.)* — how good it is to have clear fuckin' thoughts for once in my goddamn life. Instead of this dirt in my head, this trash, this confusion, this bumble, bumble of stu-

pid words like chug cock and hairy prick. God it turned me on
when you said it. I can see the words and how they made me feel,
but you knew it, didn't you? You knew it got me crazy and you
liked that. See if only I could feel like this all the time, in my nat-
ural state, if only it was this clear, I could of done something —
MARY. Me, I can't remember what it feels like, tell me, eight
months, what it feels like?
BOBBY. Remember, Mary, being there in the hall, like a bug, like
speck of dust, like moving so fast you just want a goddamn wall to
crash into, end it all?
MARY. No, tell me. Tell me. *(She closes her eyes.)*

*The Roys' kitchen ... Nancy is in the dark in the kitchen in
her pajamas; she stands at the stove staring at an empty pan,
a fried egg lying on the floor by her feet. John comes into the
room; he is in his pajamas.)*

JOHN. Nancy?
NANCY. Yeah?
JOHN. What are you doing?
NANCY. I was making an egg.
JOHN. Oh.
NANCY. Is that all right with you?
JOHN. Of course.
NANCY. Fine then, that's what I was doing, only I dropped it.
(Nancy gets on her knees, begins to pick up the egg.)
JOHN. Let me help you. *(He bends down to help her.)*
NANCY. It's okay, you don't have to help me. *(He stands.)* It's just
these stupid nonstick pans, Teflon whatever, my mother buys for
me. What if I don't want Teflon? I mean what if I want to buy my
own pans? Because I go to flip my egg, just flip it, and it slides
right out of the pan. I'm forty-three years old now, I should be able
to choose my own goddamn pan. *(She is finished cleaning; she sits.
John goes to the fridge, takes out eggs.)* What are you doing?
JOHN. I'll make you an egg.
NANCY. I don't want one anymore.

27

JOHN. Well, I could go for one, now that I'm up.

NANCY. That's not what I want. I don't want an egg. I'm sick of pretending it's about eggs, about food, about camping trips, these little things we pretend it's about. No, you know what? You're right, go ahead, make me an egg, make me an egg and everything will be fine, John.

JOHN. How do you want your egg?

NANCY. We've been married twenty years, you better know how I want my egg.

JOHN. Once over easy.

NANCY. He knows something! *(John cracks the egg; his temperature is rising.)*

JOHN. Do you want toast?

NANCY. You know I don't eat carbs, I haven't eaten carbs for two years now. I'm trying to be thin, thin and attractive, fuck it, yes! Give me toast, I want toast, I'm sick of trying. *(John gets bread, puts it in the toaster.)*

JOHN. Do you want to talk? Where is all this coming from right now? I mean, is that it? You want to talk about it, right? Because, because you could just say that, after twenty years of marriage you could say: I need to talk about it.

NANCY. Of course I don't want to talk about it, I don't want to think about it, I want it never to have happened.

JOHN. I can't go on like this.

NANCY. Well then why did you do it?

JOHN. How will we go on?

NANCY. If you wanted to go on, you wouldn't of done it.

JOHN. I should never have told you, I didn't need to tell you —

NANCY. Oh, so now you wish you had lied to me?

JOHN. No, Nancy, no. I give up, I can't keep begging you to forgive me, I can't, I can't live like this. I should go, I should just go —

NANCY. Sure, go, just throw away the last twenty years, flush them right down the toilet —

JOHN. *(Getting angry.)* I don't want to flush them down the toilet, I don't want to do that! I want to move past this, I want to talk to you, I want to erase the stupid thing I did.

NANCY. Well we can't, we can't erase. *(Liz's bedroom. Liz and Dean are in bed; they did it; her hand rests on his chest. They smile to*

28

themselves in the darkness.)

LIZ. So, now we did it.

DEAN. Yuhp.

LIZ. Nice.

DEAN. Yeah.

LIZ. You still have your boots on. I hate that.

DEAN. Happens to you a lot?

LIZ. What's that, married man?

DEAN. Ugh, very bad kids, both of us.

LIZ. Yeah … but not really bad …

DEAN. No.

LIZ. It's worse to let things get built up in your head, better to … you know.

DEAN. So we could stop wondering —

DEAN and LIZ. Right, right.

LIZ. Get it out of our system —

DEAN. Years of —

LIZ. It had to happen already.

DEAN. Now it's done.

LIZ. We can move on. *(Quiet.)* Do you love her?

DEAN. What?

LIZ. How long have you been married?

DEAN. Seven months. *(Beat.)*

LIZ. So uhmmm … Can I remove your boots?

DEAN. I should sort of go.

LIZ. Oh. *(Dean gets up, suddenly seized with guilt and desperate to get out; his pants and shoes are still on, wrapped around his ankles. He pulls them up, starts rummaging through the bed for his shirt.)* What do you do these days? You still read a lot?

DEAN. Yeah, read, work, work a lot mostly.

LIZ. Still listen to music?

DEAN. *(Looking for his shirt.)* Yeah, well, you know …

LIZ. I think about all the books and music and stuff you exposed me to, it prepared me for college more than high school did. *(Dean nods.)*

DEAN. Have you seen my shirt?

LIZ. I was studying to be, get this, a doctor.

DEAN. That's great. My shirt?

29

LIZ. Don't you think that's weird?

DEAN. What?

LIZ. Me, a doctor?

DEAN. Not really.

LIZ. I do.

DEAN. Why? It makes sense.

LIZ. What? You really could see me as a doctor?

DEAN. Look Liz, I've got responsibilities.

LIZ. Oh yeah, like cheating on your wife? *(Dean's getting mad, confused; there's a slight noise coming through the wall.)*

DEAN. I have never cheated on my wife … before, and this, fuck you, this was — just please I really want to find my shirt, will you help, please, find my shirt.

LIZ. Maybe it's in your boots!

DEAN. Thanks a lot — what's that? *(He listens, she listens, the sound of heavy breathing, moaning …)* What's that noise?

LIZ. My mom.

DEAN. Your mom is fucking fucking, holy shit, your mom is getting off.

LIZ. Shut up.

DEAN. Holy fuck, man, that is so intense, listen to her.

LIZ. Stop.

DEAN. I can't believe her room is right next to yours, she is a wild woman —

LIZ. Stop!

DEAN. That is so fucked up, mother and daughter going at it —

LIZ. Stop it!

DEAN. Hah!

LIZ. *(Over the following, the moans peter out and become quiet.)* Stop it! Stop it! She's such a fucking cunt with her stupid boyfriends and they're not even boyfriends, they don't even like her, she's just a miserable, miserable person with no, no … values, just, just this, this sponge of her own needs, and, and needs and, and I think I'm better, not better, nohoho! Stupid, ugly shit, just like her.

DEAN. *(Reaching to her.)* Liz — *(She slaps his hand away.)*

LIZ. That's why I came home you asshole, 'cause the only time I was happy, just myself, was with you! All those long stupid nights talking reading poetry bullshit with you, being a loser with you.

(She cries.)

DEAN. *(Scared.)* Don't … cry. *(Liz buries her face in her hands, weeps. Dean sits on the floor at the foot of the bed, at a loss. Bobby and Mary in the kitchen …)*

MARY. What it's like, tell me, tell me —

BOBBY. — real, actually happening, instead of this thing you walk through with all these weird faces and you're like, who the fuck is that 'cause you don't know, man. You don't know anyone and nobody knows you. But now I'm here, Mary, here, and you're there, Mary, sitting in that chair watching me and I love you, my heart's so big it's busting with love for you, and for that thing in your stomach, for your eyes, your hair, your skin, the way you smell, the way you move, like a mother, like Mother Theresa, no like Mother Earth, yeah …

MARY. Why can't he love me like that?

BOBBY. He's stupid.

MARY. Yeah. *(Bobby, crashing, lies down on the floor. Mary walks to the plate, stares at the concoction.)*

BOBBY. Whatcha doin', Mary?

MARY. Just lookin'. *(Bobby lies on the floor.)* Crashin'?

BOBBY. Yeah, owwww. *(Mary leans over, snorts the dregs of the drug left on the plate.)* Whatcha doin', Mary?

MARY. Oh god. *(Liz and Dean in the bedroom; the room is quiet now; Liz sits with her knees pulled into her chest. Dean sits near her.)*

DEAN. Sometimes I thought if you told me you were leaving, maybe I would've … *(Liz looks up at him.)* I coulda. I didn't do so bad in school, I could've done really well if I didn't have such an attitude problem. I aced the S.A.T.'s. Sometimes I fantasized I went with you to Ithaca — wherever, we'd be in your dorm room, studying on your bed, covered in books … we'd be working on some paper like about Jean-Paul Sartre's philosophy of … *(Gestures "whatever.")*

LIZ. Being and Nothingness.

DEAN. Whatever, I didn't know what I was talking about, shit, I don't even know who the fuck Jean-Paul Sartre is.

LIZ. He was a French philosopher, he had —

DEAN. Oh, please don't tell me. *(Liz smiles, a beat.)*

LIZ. You would've hated school anyway. It's sort of like a factory: You enter this teenager, all like, who the hell am I? Four years later

31

they pop you out and you don't have to worry about who you are anymore, because you're like an English major or a business major or pre-med. So even if you like work in 7-Eleven for the rest of your life you can be like: "Yeah I work in 7-Eleven, but I'm really an English major." *(They laugh.)* There was no one at school better than you. I just wish I had known that before ...

DEAN. Well, we all gotta learn however we learn, right?

LIZ. Well, I gotta learn faster then, if I keep going like this everything'll be gone by the time I figure it out. Three years of college to learn that this, you ... that I had to get back to you as soon as possible and ...

DEAN. Take on the world together!

LIZ. Yeah!

DEAN. Hey, no regrets, right? *(Liz nods.)* Shit ... Please, please just go back to school, okay? *(They look at each other, come together, begin to kiss again, getting heavy into each other. Suddenly, she slaps him away. The moans have started again, softly.)*

LIZ. Oh my god! I can't fucking believe her!

DEAN. *(Weak.)* She's doing it again?

LIZ. She wants to destroy my last shreds of dignity — let's go to your house.

DEAN. What? *(She stands.)*

LIZ. I'm not going to say anything.

DEAN. You can't.

LIZ. *(Getting hysterical again.)* I can't think in this house. I need to think, I just —

DEAN. But —

LIZ. If you care about me even the slightest —

DEAN. I do, but uhmm, Liz, uhm —

LIZ. Look, I'm not gonna destroy your perfect little marriage, if you ever had any feelings for me at all —

DEAN. I do, yes, but she's really pregnant and —

LIZ. Look, I just fucked you and I want to go to your house! *(The moans intensify.)* Ughhh! Let's go!! *(Liz storms out the door.)*

DEAN. My shirt? *(Dean picks up his jacket from the floor and runs after her. John and Nancy ...)*

JOHN. When I met you, Nance, when we met, I thought, god, we will never have enough time together. I thought, I remember

32

thinking: I wish I had met her when I was fifteen, or seven even, because it will never be enough time. *(Nancy softens, her face gives a bit.)* I feel that way still — we're wasting so much time.

NANCY. It was just hard today, to see you and the girl, a student, to watch you sing to her, and imagine ...

JOHN. It wasn't her.

NANCY. I know it wasn't her, it doesn't matter, to me they are all her, they are all her. *(John nods.)* And what's worse, I feel it all the time now with my own students. They come into the office with their searching, their questions, and I just can't look at them the same way. They were my life, John. I want to give them what I would've given my own, and now, now I look at them and see little slutty home-wreckers. I see everything weak about you, about me, about us. *(John moves his hands over his face.)* I can't help it, I can't stop thinking about it, I can't stop thinking that if we had been able to have a child, she might be that age, and you wouldn't be able to see a girl that way, not if you had your own. But I have to stop thinking like that, I have to stop saying things like "if we had," we couldn't ... I have to get past, I need to, tell me how, please? Tell me, I beg you. Tell me how to get past it, John?

JOHN. Oh god, I wish I knew. *(Blackout.)*

Scene 5

Dean's kitchen ... about fifteen minutes later. Dean stares at the drug plate. Bobby sits on the floor. Mary stands, staring, frightened, at Dean. Liz stands staring at Mary, taking in the decrepit kitchen ...

DEAN. You didn't. You didn't do this.

MARY. You guys are home awful late.

DEAN. Did you guys do this?

BOBBY. Hey, Liz.

LIZ. Hi. Hey, Mary, it's been a long time, wow, wow. God, you're

33

big.

MARY. Screw you.

LIZ. I'm sorry, I didn't mean it like — it's just you're really having a baby — it's nice to see you, Mary.

DEAN. How come you're not in the room? How come she's not in the room, Bob?

LIZ. What's the room?

MARY. It's four in the morning, why is she here?

BOBBY. It's cool, Dean.

LIZ. We were just talking and talking, totally lost track of time.

DEAN. Jesus man —

BOBBY. Seriously, I just let her out.

LIZ. Let her out of where?

MARY. What do you care anyway? What is she doing here?

DEAN. We're just friends.

MARY. And Bobby just let me out of the room.

LIZ. You guys make it sound like you keep her locked up.

MARY. Well, they do.

DEAN. Bobby just let you out?

LIZ. That's awful strange, you guys.

DEAN. Just now?

BOBBY. Yeah man, c'mon.

LIZ. Mary, Dean locks you up?

MARY. Yeah, locked up in a room all the time so he can hang out with whores like you.

DEAN. What are you talking about? I never go out.

LIZ. Are you literally locked up?

MARY. Literally, yeah literally, show her the key, Bobby, show her the key. *(Bobby dangles the key that hangs from a string around his neck.)*

DEAN. Oh man, I don't believe you did this, how could you, Mary?

LIZ. Dean, you lock her up?

MARY. Mind your own business.

LIZ. That is very disturbing —

DEAN. Stay out of this, Liz. *(To Mary.)* I'm gonna call your fucking dad —

MARY. Oh good, so he can beat me? He doesn't care and you don't care.

DEAN. What is wrong with you?

LIZ. Look, Dean, she can't help it, it's addiction. I was pre-med —

MARY. Oh thank you, Liz! *(Mary walks to Dean, pulls open his jacket.)* Where's your shirt, Dean? *(Dean is silent.)* Where? Where is it?

LIZ. It got wet.

MARY. I want him to tell me. Where is it? *(Her gaze is penetrating ...)*

DEAN. I, I spilled ... on it.

MARY. Yeah, I did it.

DEAN. Mother Fucker Jesus Fucking Christ, Bob.

BOBBY. It's not my fault, Dean —

LIZ. What happened to you guys?

DEAN. I can't believe this.

LIZ. Living like this — *(Dean starts to kick things.)*

MARY. Great! Now he's losing it.

LIZ. Oh Dean, be careful, look, let's all calm down, okay?

BOBBY. I swear, Dean —

LIZ. Dean, stop it! Stop it! This is a serious situation and you have to start behaving like an adult here —

MARY. Uh-oh, look at him — *(Mary cowers.)*

DEAN. I'm an adult, I'm fucking adult, I work forty hours a week, I'm married, I'm having a baby, I support you guys, clothes, health insurance, food. I can't even come home to a fucking meal, a conversation, I'm too tired to read a goddamn book, just come home, drink a beer, put the TV on, sounds like an adult to me! *(Dean kicks the stove.)*

LIZ. Yes, you're an adult, relax, okay? Sit! Sit! *(Dean sits.)* Good! All right, okay. Mary had a little relapse tonight, okay, she was angry, but maybe this needed to happen —

MARY. You don't know anything, nothing, you don't live here, get out of my house —

LIZ. Mary, they lock you up!

MARY. Well, I want them to! *(Mary rubs her stomach lovingly.)* I want them to.

DEAN. What the fuck, Mare? One night, one night and everything falls apart.

MARY. I'm sorry, Dean.

DEAN. I can't do this, all the time, I need a life too, you know, I'm a fucking person too. You, Bobby, I support, I pay for your shoes, your tapes, your video games.

BOBBY. It's not my fault.

DEAN. Well whose fucking fault is it? Huh? Whose? It all sucks man, I should just blow my brains out.

LIZ. No one is going to blow their brains out, okay?

BOBBY. I would never let Mary get hurt. I love Mary.

LIZ. Okay?

DEAN. Shut up, Bobby, shut up before I fuckin' kill you! Goddammit!

BOBBY. I swear, Dean.

DEAN. You think I'm stupid? It's gonna die now.

MARY. IT! IT!

BOBBY. C'mon, Dean, man —

DEAN. Mother! FUCK! *(Dean kicks over the table; everyone cowers.)*

MARY. Oh no!

BOBBY. Dean, c'mon —

LIZ. Dean, what happened to you? *(Dean begins freaking out, knocking things around. Everyone cowers.)* What's he doing?

MARY. He's losing his temper! *(Dean trashes the kitchen. Everyone crouches down, covering their heads. Dean throws pots and pans, knocks over the kitchen table, the garbage, grabs a package of spaghetti, smashes it down on the counter; some of the spaghetti goes flying around the room; the rest of it slides out of his hands onto the floor, Dean, out of steam, slides with it. He falls to the floor and rocks himself. Quiet moments pass.)*

LIZ. Is everyone okay?

BOBBY. He has a lot of pressure … *(They all sit quietly; Liz looks over at Mary, who is holding her stomach tenderly.)*

LIZ. What's it like?

MARY. What?

LIZ. You know, having a baby?

MARY. Ohh, it's like having the sun, inside you.

LIZ. Can I? Can I touch it?

MARY. What?

LIZ. Does it kick?

MARY. Yeah.

36

LIZ. C'I touch it? *(Liz crawls to Mary, and puts her hands on her stomach.)* Wow.

MARY. Can you feel it? *(Liz nods yes.)* Neat huh?

LIZ. I'd like to be in there.

BOBBY. Let's all be quiet now.

MARY. It's really hard, Dean, I know, 'specially 'cause we have no one to talk to.

LIZ. You just have to trust yourselves. *(They look at Liz.)* We have all the answers, everything we need, inside of us already, we just have to have faith.

DEAN. Where'd you get that? A fortune cookie?

LIZ. No, Mr. Roy said that.

MARY. The guidance counselor?

LIZ. I saw him when I was at work the other day. He was so great and wise in high school, you should talk to him, he made me feel really special, he would say: You can do anything.

MARY. He was pretty nice, I guess.

DEAN. What a crock, corny crock.

MARY. I love you, Dean.

DEAN. Great.

BOBBY. Guys?

MARY. I always loved you, since second grade, and I didn't care if you loved Liz —

LIZ. Oh, he doesn't love me.

MARY. You let me down tonight, too, Dean.

BOBBY. All right guys, I'm gonna make my way out of the room — *(Bobby begins to pull himself weakly towards the doorway. Liz looks over at Mary, notices something.)*

LIZ. Mary?

MARY. What?

LIZ. Mary? I think ...

MARY. Yeah?

LIZ. I think there's water coming between your legs. Don't you feel something? *(Liz lifts her hand to the room; it's wet and glistening with water.)*

BOBBY. No way, no way —

MARY. Oh god, Dean.

DEAN. This it?

37

MARY. Yeah? Oh gosh, what should I do?

LIZ. We should go to the hospital.

MARY. *(Labor pains.)* I feel it, now I feel it, oh, now I feel it.

DEAN. Mary?

LIZ. Guys —

BOBBY. Wet? It's wet?

DEAN. It's time? *(Liz stands.)*

LIZ. Let's go to the hospital.

MARY. Dean? *(Mary reaches her hand out to him — Liz watches, Bobby watches. Dean goes to Mary, takes her hand.)* It's here!

DEAN. It is?

LIZ. Let's go to the hospital!!

MARY. We're having a baby, Dean.

BOBBY. OH WOWWW!!!! *(Blackout.)*

ACT TWO

In black, the sound of a newborn baby crying.

Scene 1

Four days later. Morning ... Liz stands in the kitchen of John and Nancy Roy's kitchen. There is stuff packed by the door for the Roys' camping trip.

LIZ. We met the other day in Anakonda — Liz ... Mr. Roy, he was my guidance counselor. I just wanted to ask — talk to him about something ... he was just so helpful in high school and ...
NANCY. I see.
LIZ. Yeah.
NANCY. Can I get you something to drink?
LIZ. Okay, I'll have some water. *(Nancy gets water.)* I'm kind of dehydrated. It's really hot.
NANCY. Yes it is. Here.
LIZ. Thanks. I can't believe it's this hot already. *(Liz gulps down water. Nancy watches her.)*
NANCY. Would you like another glass?
LIZ. Well ... if it's no problem ...
NANCY. No problem, no problem at all. *(Nancy gets Liz another glass of water.)*
LIZ. I was the sales girl, remember? In Anakonda Kaye Sports...?
NANCY. *(Nods.)* You dropped out of Ithaca.
LIZ. That's right, that was me. *(An uncomfortable silence fills the room, finally ...)*

LIZ.	NANCY.
Do you have — ?	What are your — ?

NANCY. Go ahead —

LIZ. No, you —

NANCY. No, no I didn't really have anything to say.

LIZ. Me either, really, it just looks like you're going camping so, I was just gonna ask where?

NANCY. We're going on vacation to Maine.

LIZ. Oh nice.

NANCY. We're leaving later today, driving into the sunset. Bar Harbor.

LIZ. Oh, I've heard it's just beautiful.

NANCY. We haven't been on vacation in years, I can't wait, we'll rent bikes, eat lobster, fudge …

LIZ. That sounds so great.

NANCY. Yes.

LIZ. Cool. *(They stand there. Nancy watches Liz. Liz is uncomfortable.)* So uhm, is he here? Mr. Roy?

NANCY. He's on the toilet.

LIZ. Oh.

NANCY. He takes the paper in with him.

LIZ. Oh.

NANCY. He could be out any minute now, or he could be an hour.

LIZ. Okay.

NANCY. You could sit.

LIZ. Oh, I'm cool.

NANCY. You sure?

LIZ. Yeah. *(Beat.)*

NANCY. So, Mr. Roy, he made an impression on you?

LIZ. He was wonderful.

NANCY. Did you spend a lot of time in his office?

LIZ. Well, I guess, I mean the regular amount of time I guess, maybe more. I thought he was the coolest.

NANCY. The coolest?

LIZ. Oh totally. I mean not a lot of teachers care, but he did. I think, you know, he spotted that I wanted more from life, and you know, he nurtured that.

NANCY. Of course he did.

LIZ. Yeah. *(John enters with the paper.)*

NANCY. Oh look, it's Mr. Roy.

LIZ. Hey Mr. Roy.

JOHN. Hey. *(He looks at his wife.)*

NANCY. Well, I'll let you two catch up. *(She gets up.)*

JOHN. Oh.

NANCY. I'll be in the shower, or should I wait?

JOHN. What?

NANCY. Does it smell?

JOHN. *(Laughs uncomfortably.)* It's fine. *(John sits at the table, puts the paper down. Nancy goes to leave.)* See ya, Nance. *(She leaves. Liz smiles at John. He smiles back.)* Hey kid, nice surprise, you look great.

LIZ. Thanks.

MR. ROY. How's it going? *(Liz shakes her head. Her eyes drop to the floor.)*

JOHN. I was thinking about, about your choice, to, uhmm, take some time off. I think it's really brave and smart. We're so, uhmm, conditioned: graduate high school, go to college, get a job. I was getting ready to go to college in the late sixties when personal time, anti-establishment behavior was embraced.

LIZ. *(Quiet.)* I didn't drop ...

JOHN. What?

LIZ. I did, but I didn't.

JOHN. Something happen? At school? You got...?

LIZ. I can't go back.

JOHN. You were...?

LIZ. I couldn't make it.

JOHN. The work?

LIZ. Yes ... no.

JOHN. God, we just don't have the resources to prepare you kids, it infuriates —

LIZ. I do things.

JOHN. Things?

LIZ. Stupid things, dumb things, betray myself.

JOHN. Betray?

LIZ. To be liked, to be, to be someone.

JOHN. I'm not quite following you, kid.

LIZ. People know, they know and they take advantage. One time there was this piece of pizza on the ground, like a car had run over

41

it, and they all bet how little they'd have to pay me to eat it. I ate it for five dollars. *(She looks up at him. Her eyes have begun to tear.)* Why? Why, Mr. Roy? *(He nods.)*

JOHN. So you didn't drop out?

LIZ. I can't go back. *(She begins to cry.)*

JOHN. Oh, gosh, oh don't cry. *(He looks around worried that Nancy may walk in.)*

LIZ. I am so totally lost.

JOHN. Well, we all lose our way from time to time, but we find it again.

LIZ. And see there was one thing, one person in this whole stupid life who loved me, who I loved and I left him, now I've lost that, him. Can you imagine? Do you even understand what that's like? To lose the only thing? *(John nods.)* You do? *(John nods again.)* Why? What is it? That some people just have this need, this like force like inside them that makes them, ya know, lose? *(He shrugs. Liz shakes her head, desperate to hold back the tears.)*

JOHN. I don't know what it is, God I wish I knew. But you're right, there's something inside of us, some of us, that, that wants to destroy the little bit of meaning. I love my marriage. So little in life means something. Nancy and 1, we have no children, last year was bad, I drank a lot, I almost lost everything. I almost lost my wife, now I have to fight for it, my marriage. You're a smart girl Liz, that's why I feel like I can tell you this. *(Liz listens.)* Something went wrong with me and Nancy, and I know she thought, we thought, if we had been able to have a child it, we thought, that, that inability to progress is what soured it. But, you got to step up to the plate and accept life on life's terms. Work, work to fix it, fight for it, fight to hold onto the things in life that mean, that's what we have to do. Does anything I say make any sense?

LIZ. Yeah, but how?

JOHN. Well kid, that's the challenge, isn't it?

LIZ. How do you fix the fact that you can't have a child? That I can't have what I want? *(John shakes his head. He doesn't know. Liz looks up suddenly.)* Help me, Mr. Roy?

JOHN. H — how?

LIZ. Please — *(John comes toward her. His heart aches for her. Nancy enters the room.)*

NANCY. Ahem. You're still here? *(John backs away from Liz.)*
LIZ. Yeah.
JOHN. Liz is uhmmm looking for help.
NANCY. With what?
LIZ. It's complicated. I just thought, Mr. Roy, he knew me …
NANCY. Yes?
JOHN. I think, tell us, Liz —
NANCY. Yes, what do you need help with, Liz? *(Liz blushes deep red.)*
LIZ. *(Mumbles at her shoes.)* Just what to do, ya know, with my life —
NANCY. I can't hear you.
LIZ. I don't know, it's stupid.
NANCY. Well then there you have it.
JOHN. Hold on, Nance —
LIZ. Just forget it.
JOHN. No, it's okay, kid, if there's something you need —
NANCY. Look, Liz —
JOHN. Nance —
NANCY. No, you have come to two people who work ruthlessly to better the lives of young people. I work in the Albany inner-city school system. I have 100 sixteen, seventeen-year-old kids who can't read past the second grade. These kids, they live in a sea of opposition, there is no Ithaca for them, no pre-med, no boyfriends at Cornell, I mean, what will happen to them? What will happen to those kids? I give them as much as I can, but it's not enough. It's summer break, we are on vacation, John has … every day is a struggle for me, for him. We give our time, our hearts to the people who need us most, we could not have children of our own, so we have dedicated our lives to these kids. What I'm asking you, Liz, and I'm asking with the deepest concern and sincerity, do you need our help? Because we need time right now, for us. *(She looks at her husband. He nods. Beat.)*
LIZ. Thank you, no, I get it. I understand. Thank you for listening, your time. I understand. Thank you for your time. Bye! *(Liz runs out of the kitchen. John and Nancy look after her, then at each other.)*
NANCY. Was I…? *(Shakes his head no. Half smiles at her.)*
JOHN. No. *(They look at each other. Silence and emptiness fill the space between them. Blackout.)*

43

Scene 2

Dean's kitchen, a little later. Liz stands in the kitchen; she has come directly from the Roys'. She is shaky, excited, but tentative. Dean is sitting on the kitchen table, drinking.

LIZ. Dean, I have something I want to tell you, see, I've had something of a revelation and I want to say it, even though it may sound terrifying, but it's the last thing I'll say, so, so knowing that ... you can tell me to leave, you can say: There is nothing you could say, Liz, that I would possibly want to hear —
DEAN. Shh ... they're sleeping. *(She comes to him, purpose in her step, sits beside him.)*
LIZ. Why are you home anyway?
DEAN. I took a half day. *(Clutches his stomach.)* Ugh.
LIZ. You okay?
DEAN. I can't believe they just let you take it home, you know? Just like that, just ...
LIZ. I know.
DEAN. No instructions, no certificate, in and out and there you have it, you know?
LIZ. It's ... *(She shakes her head, baffled.)*
DEAN. Want some? *(She looks at the bottle,)*
LIZ. It's not the way to deal with it.
DEAN. Oh, Liz.
LIZ. What?
DEAN. The last few nights have been ... I come home from work, this place, my house, and I tiptoe because ... I look at Mary lying with it in the bed, staring at it, her eyes like, like pow, and I want to see it that way ...
LIZ. That's part of what I want to ... See I went to Mr. Roy's this morning, before I came here, I just was feeling so ... I wanted some advice, whatever.
DEAN. He give you some?

44

LIZ. He and his wife are these amazing people, she works in the inner-city school system with all these kids who can't even read. They give so much to these kids because they have a hole in their lives, they couldn't have a baby.

DEAN. Like I love to say ... one man's dream ...

LIZ. Yes, this is, this is where I'm getting to —

DEAN. It's just the baby, it's so soft and small, ya know? Her skin, wow, shit fuck, ya know. I can't touch a thing like that, ya know? *(Quiet.)*

LIZ. I can't stop thinking about it either. That night, Mary's stomach, the sound of crying, new life ... we were once that, Dean, babies, and our parents, they were ... like us, and they ...

DEAN. Fucked up. *(Beat; they nod at each other.)*

LIZ. I have an idea of something we can do that's good, but I don't want to make things worse.

DEAN. I'm glad you're here.

LIZ. Really?

DEAN. I need you.

LIZ. You do? *(He nods. She takes his hand; they hold on to each other tightly.)*

DEAN. I don't know what to do?

LIZ. I think you have to ask yourself, can you do it?

DEAN. What?

LIZ. Be a dad?

DEAN. I have to.

LIZ. Dean, my mom didn't want a kid ... it's not good ... *(Dean looks at her.)*

DEAN. Guess what I got on the S.A.T.'s?

LIZ. I have no idea.

DEAN. 1370.

LIZ. No way.

DEAN. I'll show you.

LIZ. It's okay —

DEAN. No, I want you to see this ... *(He leaves. Bobby enters, quietly, he is a little luded out.)*

BOBBY. Hey, Liz.

LIZ. Hey, Bobby.

BOBBY. Where's the baby?

LIZ. I think it's sleeping.

BOBBY. Aw phew, it's crying really freaks me out. I mean it's exciting, but just sometimes, the crying, it freaks me out.

LIZ. Yeah.

BOBBY. 'Cause it's like goodness, ya know? It like makes you want to be a better person, ya know?

LIZ. Then you should try.

BOBBY. What?

LIZ. Being a better person, chill on the stuff.

BOBBY. *(Defensive.)* Ughhh ... I wanna be good, Liz, but it's my life, mine, what I chose to do.

LIZ. Oh god, Bobby. *(Dean enters the room with his S.A.T. scores.)*

DEAN. Here, my fucking S.A.T. scores! See that! See that!

BOBBY. Dean scored 1380.

DEAN. 70, 1370.

BOBBY. Oh right.

LIZ. Wow, you did. I mean I know you're smart, but this is amazing. I always said.

BOBBY. Oh shit, the baby is so intense —

DEAN. That's the thing, I am smart, I am. Huh, you didn't believe me when I said I could go to Ithaca —

LIZ. I did, I knew you could go to Ithaca, I mean with these scores you could go to Cornell!

BOBBY. So intense.

DEAN. But I didn't.

LIZ. You still could.

DEAN. Fuck it. I just had a baby, my life is over, man. It's fine, I can accept responsibility, I understand what it is, but shit, I coulda.

BOBBY. I don't think I could stop, and it's not my fault, it's my brain, something's wrong in my brain.

LIZ. I can't stand what's happened to you —

DEAN. Nothing has happened to me! This is what I chose.

LIZ. You choose to work forty hours a week? Support everyone? Have no time to read, just drink beer, turn the TV on?!? You're, you're gonna end up dying one of the people we never wanted to be. You know how many people want a baby? People like the Roys', people whose lives would have meaning, value, give value, make that baby valuable.

46

DEAN. What are you saying, Liz? Give it up? Like drop it on someone's doorstep? Give it to the Roys? What?

BOBBY. The Roys want a baby? *(Quiet.)*

LIZ. Yes. Yes, the Roys do want a baby.

DEAN. We can't just give our baby to the Roys.

LIZ. Can't you? Why not? The Roys could, and we could do something, own our lives, give that baby a chance to own its life — because it doesn't have to be this way, not if we, if we ... progress! *(She looks at Dean; he is speechless.)*

BOBBY. Whoa, Liz, are you saying what I think you're saying? *(Liz and Dean look at each other.)* Whoa. *(Mary enters with the baby, holding it close to her body.)*

MARY. Pollyanna! Guys, Pollyanna, isn't that a good name? It's a movie I saw when I was a kid about this girl named Pollyanna, so nice. She falls out of a tree. But this Pollyanna won't. Whaddya think? *(They all stare at her.)* Of the name? Whaddya think?

DEAN. *(Slowly.)* It's nice.

MARY. Yeah. Look at her, just look at her, she's definitely special. Look how perfect. I can't believe it. *(Tears well up in Mary's eyes.)* I've never seen anything so beautiful, and I made her, she's mine, she comes from me! *(Mary looks up at them, her face shining. She looks around the kitchen, taking in the mess.)* Oh my god. You guys, we gotta clean, we've gotta scrub. We can't let Pollyana grow up like this! I told you guys, didn't I? I said things were gonna change. We're gonna get our shit together! *(Mary approaches Bobby, who is sitting on the floor.)* That means you too, Bobby, no more of that shit, I don't want it around me, or the baby.

BOBBY. But Mary —

MARY. Look, if I can —

LIZ. But can you?

MARY. What?

DEAN. *(Timid.)* We have to ask.

MARY. What?

LIZ. If you can, Mary? For the baby.

MARY. What are you doing? Why is she saying that?

LIZ. Mary, listen, they've had you locked up in that room for eight months, you can't stay locked up forever.

MARY. If it's not around I won't do it. Mind your own business,

Dean, tell her to mind her own business.

DEAN. Listen Mary, baby —

MARY. What?

DEAN. I mean, look, she's a little right, It's been four days, and
we still lock you up when I go to work, and that's a pretty weird
way to raise a baby, right?

MARY. You haven't given me a chance.

DEAN. And look at this place, can we, ya know? Should we?

MARY. What are you saying, Dean? How could you even, Dean?
Why are you guys doing this to me?

LIZ. We're not doing anything, Mary. I know what it is to be
Pollyanna —

MARY. Look at her, Dean, just look — *(Mary brings the baby to
Dean, parts the blanket around her face.)* Look how beautiful.
That's us, Dean. You and me. Even if you don't love me, look what
we did, together. It's amazing. *(Dean stares. Mary looks at him. His
eyes are glazed over.)* You don't like her.

DEAN. No, it's not that.

MARY. Bobby?

BOBBY. Yeah, Mary?

MARY. What's going on?

BOBBY. I donno, I wish I knew.

LIZ. Sometimes it's hard to see things on the inside, when it's you,
sometimes it's hard to see, but I look, from the outside and I ask,
I feel obligated to ask, can you stop, Mary? *(Mary holds Pollyanna
tightly to her chest.)*

MARY. I want to. I want to. Oh god, I want to.

LIZ. Of course you do, Mary.

BOBBY. We could try.

LIZ. What?

BOBBY. Like an experiment.

DEAN. What, Bobby?

BOBBY. I got some rock, in my pocket.

MARY. You do?

LIZ. No.

DEAN. Not a good idea.

BOBBY. But then we'd know —

DEAN. Know what?

BOBBY. If we should give the baby to Mr. Roy. *(Beat.)*
MARY. What?
LIZ. Bobby!
DEAN. Shit, Bob —
MARY. What?
BOBBY. I just thought if I put some on the table, we could see if Mary could stop, then we'd know.
MARY. What's this got to do with Mr. Roy?
DEAN. Nothing.
MARY. Tell me.
DEAN. Just he wants a baby.
MARY. You want me to give Pollyanna to Mr. Roy?
DEAN. No. I just thought, I got this feeling, when it came, and then these last four days, when it cries, when I look at it —
MARY. Stop calling her "it!" Her name is Pollyanna.
DEAN. Pollyanna, okay. I was like, well, things went through my head, things like, shit I've never been anywhere. Like Mary, remember we used to talk about taking a road trip? Driving cross-country together?
MARY. Yeah, but we could do that with Polly, we could still do it.
DEAN. But stuff went through my head, stuff like that, and I remembered how all the teachers in high school thought I was a dumb-ass and then I got a 1370 on the S.A.T.'s ... So, maybe it's not right to do this, if we, if we can't, if we're not ready. *(Beat.)*
MARY. Put the rock out.
BOBBY. What?
MARY. Put it out. Put it on the table —
LIZ. That's not the point, Mary, you don't have to do that —
MARY. What is the point then, huh? Put it out, Bobby, you'll see, you'll all see, put it out. Do it! *(Bobby stands and puts a gleaming white rock on the table; they all look at it.)*
BOBBY. You can do it, Mary, I know you can.
MARY. Thanks, Bob, obviously you're the only one who believes in me.
LIZ. This isn't what I had in mind. This isn't a good idea.
DEAN. Maybe it is.
MARY. Yeah, maybe it is. I'm so sick of all of you acting like my dad, he never believed in me. Now, all I have to do is look at Polly

49

and I believe in myself. *(Mary sits at the table holding Polly tightly to her chest. She looks at the rock; she looks at Pollyanna; it's hard.)* Now let's make a meal like a normal family. Whaddya want to eat?

DEAN. *(Stares at Mary, his S.A.T. scores held limply in his hand.)* Anything.

MARY. Who's gonna help me? I can't really hold Polly and cook.

BOBBY. I will.

LIZ. I'll help too.

MARY. There's some spaghetti in that top cabinet and a jar of sauce. *(Bobby goes to the cabinet, pulls down the pasta and sauce.)*

BOBBY. Okay, got it. Got it. *(Liz goes to the sink, makes a pot of water.)*

MARY. Are there any vegetables in the fridge? Will someone look? *(Liz goes to the fridge, looks. Mary stares at the rock, then back at Pollyanna; she starts to sweat.)*

LIZ. No.

MARY. Well, from now on, from now on we'll have vegetables. Right, Dean?

DEAN. Uh-huh.

BOBBY. Okay, Liz, you take over for a sec.

LIZ. Sure. *(Bobby goes to the rock, scrapes some off, Mary watches. Trying to distract Mary:)* I always wanted to eat as a family, if I ever have kids I'm gonna make sure it's a rule, that we always have meals together. *(Bobby leaves the room.)* It's important, ritual, doing things together, as a family, I didn't have that. Are there any spices? Pepper? *(Liz looks in cabinets.)*

MARY. *(Quietly.)* Oh god.

DEAN. Mary?

LIZ. I could do this every day, be normal, little stupid things every day: work, cook —

MARY. I can't, I can't.

DEAN. Liz? *(She turns to them.)*

MARY. I can't, Dean, I can't —

DEAN. Bobby!!!

MARY. *(Starting to cry.)* I can't do it.

LIZ. You can't?

MARY. No, no, I can't do it, get it away, oh darn. Get it away! *(Mary pushes the rock off the table onto the floor.)*

DEAN. *(Calls off.)* Bobby!!!

MARY. I love Polly, I love her, but I can't, not by myself, oh Liz, Dean? Someone help me?

BOBBY. *(On his knees, looking for the rock.)* It's the worst, Mary, the worst thing in the whole world, I wish I never tried it, I wish I never did, I totally understand though, Mary. I totally know what it's like.

LIZ. We'll go to the Roys'.

MARY. What's so much better about the Roys than me? *(Looks at Dean.)* Dean?

DEAN. I ... I ...

MARY. Help me, Dean.

DEAN. I'm sorry, Mary, I don't, I don't know ... *(Blackout.)*

Scene 3

The Roys' kitchen. Mary holds Pollyanna (who is very well wrapped in lots of blankets.) Dean, Liz and Bobby stand in the kitchen. John and Nancy stare at them. Two packed suitcases sit on the floor.

JOHN. Hey kids. We were about to leave for Maine.

BOBBY. Hey, Mr. Roy, cool to see you.

JOHN. Yes. Yes, you too, kid. Liz buddy, hey, and, and ...

LIZ. Mary.

JOHN. Mary, of course. And you're, you're ...

LIZ and DEAN. Dean.

JOHN. That's right. You surprised us all with very high S.A.T. scores, I remember that.

DEAN. *(Smiles, shrugs, looks at his feet.)* Yeah.

JOHN. Well, this is my wife, Nancy.

DEAN, BOBBY and MARY. Hi.

NANCY. Hello.

LIZ. We were just wondering if we could get a second of your time.

JOHN. Well, we're about to leave.

LIZ. Just a second.

JOHN. If it's really just a second.

NANCY. I'll wait in the car.

LIZ. No, you should stay, it involves you too.

NANCY. But Liz, I thought we — we're going on vacation.

LIZ. It's a really quick idea I had, it'll only take a moment, you might want to sit down though, it's actually not that quick of an idea, I mean, it's quick to say, but long maybe to digest.

JOHN. I just wanted to get on the road by five o'clock, before traffic gets too heavy.

NANCY. I can't believe this. Don't you kids know why one teaches high school? Works in the public school system? Summers off, vacation. I believe it's June, June — summer — summer — vacation. *(Mary backs up slowly, she squeezes Pollyanna into her chest.)*

JOHN. *(Annoyed.)* Let's just give them a second, Nancy.

NANCY. Oh but it's always just a second.

LIZ. I think it's worth your time, Mrs Roy.

NANCY. I want to go on this vacation. I want to hike, I want to be with my husband.

JOHN. Okay, we'll go. Sorry kids. When I get back I would love to sit down with all of you and check in. *(The kids look up at John and Nancy devastated. Pollyanna cries.)*

MARY. I think she wet herself. *(Nancy stops.)*

NANCY. Do you need to change her?

MARY. Thanks. I guess I should ... *(Nancy comes to Mary, peeks into the blanket.)*

NANCY. Oh god, she's beautiful, she can't be more than ...

MARY. Four days.

NANCY. Four days?!? Oh look, how beautiful. John come, come, look at her she's precious. Four days old. *(John comes; he looks; he smiles.)*

JOHN. Yes she is. *(He touches Nancy lightly on the back, subconsciously.)*

NANCY. We can change her on the bed, come with me. *(Nancy leads Mary out of the room.)*

LIZ. See, I knew it! This is it, this is the thing, c'mon guys, admit it! This is it!

BOBBY. Yeah, wow. *(Dean stares at his shoes.)*

JOHN. Why's that?

LIZ. *(Full of pride.)* Well … we want you guys to have the baby. *(Beat.)*

JOHN. What?

LIZ. See, Mary and Dean, they're thinking that they're not ready to be parents. Right, Dean?

DEAN. Yeah.

LIZ. And you and Mrs. Roy, I could feel it, when I was here, this morning, I always thought you would be the best dad, and I know right now you're in a tough spot, well, maybe the baby, the baby —

JOHN. Oh. Oh no. I don't … you want to give us your baby?

LIZ. Yes!

DEAN. Mary calls her Pollyanna.

BOBBY. She's pretty cute. *(Nancy comes back into the kitchen; she is holding Pollyanna to her body.)*

NANCY. Mary'll be right out, she's in the bathroom. Gorgeous, just beautiful, you kids are very lucky, very lucky.

DEAN. Yeah. *(Nancy brings the baby to Dean, holds Pollyanna out for him to take. He stands there awkwardly, reaches his arms out. Nancy gently places her in Dean's arms. He holds her.)*

NANCY. Oops, watch her head. *(She guides Dean's arms.)* Babies have very delicate heads. *(Dean stares at Pollyanna; she gurgles. He smiles at her.)*

DEAN. Hey guys, you see that? She smiled.

NANCY. You're her dad.

DEAN. Wow. Shit. Oops. No cursing, right? *(Nancy and John laugh; John touches Nancy's shoulder.)* Hey, hey Pollyanna, hey. Hahahaha. *(Bobby comes to Dean, looks at Pollyanna.)*

BOBBY. She's smiling at you, Dean.

DEAN. Yeah.

BOBBY. Cute. Heehee cute.

DEAN. Yeah, she likes me.

LIZ. Babies don't smile at four days old, Dean.

DEAN. She's smiling at me.

LIZ. I was pre-med, it's gas, Dean, it's passing gas. *(Dean looks up, questioning, at Nancy.)*

NANCY. Well, yes, that's true, but soon she will be, she'll be smiling all the time, at her dad.

DEAN. Well, I think she's smiling now. *(Pollyanna starts to cry; Dean gets nervous.)* Oops, what'd I do? What'd I do? *(Nancy takes Pollyanna from Dean, holds her. Pollyanna stops whimpering.)* Did I do something?

NANCY. Babies are incredibly perceptive, they can sense the slightest inkling of fear, or lack of confidence.

LIZ. The baby knows Dean. *(Mary returns from the bathroom, sees Nancy holding her baby lovingly. Watches her.)*

MARY. Nancy was really good with the baby, she knew how to change her and everything.

NANCY. I love children.

MARY. How do you know how to do all that stuff?

NANCY. I babysat.

MARY. Oh. I never did.

NANCY. You'll have instincts.

MARY. My instincts are kinda fucked.

DEAN. No cursing.

MARY. What?

DEAN. Around the baby.

MARY. Oh.

LIZ. We came to see if you guys wanted her —

DEAN. To take care of her, because we were thinking we might not be ready ...

NANCY. What?

LIZ. They're just not ready.

MARY. We weren't sure ...

NANCY. What?

JOHN. They say they want to give her to us.

NANCY. Pollyanna?

LIZ. Yes!

NANCY. Why?

MARY. I got this problem.

DEAN. We're really scared.

MARY. Liz thought —

LIZ. It's a miracle, don't you think?

JOHN. Well, I'm not quite sure, miracle?

NANCY. What kind of problem?

MARY. *(Under her breath.)* Drugs.

NANCY. What?

MARY. Anything speedy, really.

NANCY. That's a problem.

JOHN. That's intense, kid. You, Dean?

DEAN. No.

LIZ. So, you see, it's perfect, isn't it? I mean I knew, Mrs. Roy, my mother wasn't ready, and so she couldn't love me completely —

MARY. I love her completely.

LIZ. So I can't love myself, not completely.

DEAN. You do, Mary.

MARY. Do you, Dean? Do you love her?

DEAN. Maybe, maybe I do ... ?

MARY. We made that together, how could you not love her?

NANCY. What you're telling me is that you have a drug problem and you're afraid you can't take care of her properly.

MARY. But I want to.

JOHN. We know you want to.

MARY. I want to so bad, so bad.

JOHN. Yes, we know.

NANCY. We know. I just want to get the facts.

BOBBY. The facts, the facts.

MARY. Liz doesn't think I can.

LIZ. It's not about you, Mary —

MARY. Just because your mother couldn't.

LIZ. It's the right thing, Mary, I know, I know — you understand what I'm trying to do, Mr. Roy? *(He shakes his head no.)* Mrs. Roy?

NANCY. If you need time ... time to get Mary help ... we'll take her —

JOHN. Nancy —

NANCY. What?

JOHN. I just ...

NANCY. Just what? Just what, John?

MARY. Dean?

DEAN. Yeah?

MARY. Can't we think about it a little more?

LIZ. I can't believe you guys, think about the baby!

DEAN. I'm thinking about her, I'm thinking about my baby —

LIZ. Think about yourself, Dean.

DEAN. I am.

NANCY. Just until Mary's ... recovered.

JOHN. Nance, let's slow down here, talk this through.

NANCY. We would do that. We would take care of her, aren't you afraid for the future of this child?

JOHN. Of course.

LIZ. Your future, Dean, you are in such total denial —

DEAN. Stop it, just stop it, it's our decision, ours, so please, please Liz, stop! *(Liz shakes her head, incredulous.)*

MARY. *(To the Roys.)* I just want to think about it a little more. *(Mary runs to Nancy, takes the baby out of her arms. Nancy does not want to let go.)*

NANCY. If you have a drug problem you cannot raise a child.

LIZ. That's what I've been trying to tell them.

BOBBY. Mary takes good care of me.

JOHN. All that I'm saying is that we should make sure we cover all the bases.

NANCY. God, you are such a liberal. You know how many families would give anything for a beautiful, healthy child, this child could have anything, are you going to keep her from that?

JOHN. That's not the point.

BOBBY. I'm just gonna go in the bathroom for a sec. *(He leaves.)*

NANCY. What is the point then?

JOHN. Well, the point is that Mary and Dean need to sit down and make an informed decision —

NANCY. Liz?

LIZ. Yeah?

NANCY. This was your idea, right?

LIZ. Yes.

NANCY. Your mother, she, she wasn't equipped, right?

LIZ. *(Wavering.)* I guess.

NANCY. She wasn't ready —

JOHN. Nancy —

LIZ. *(Shrugs.)* Yeah.

MARY. Just because your mom wasn't —

LIZ. Neither are you, neither is Dean —

JOHN. This is not the way, we've all got —

NANCY. No? What is the way, John? I've stood by you through it all, through it all, John, through your indecision, your depression, your drinking, it's my turn now, John, mine!

JOHN. Oh, Nancy.

NANCY. Imagine, Liz, imagine who you might have been if you had had better, no, parents more equipped, you're a super smart girl right, you go to Ithaca, right? But I'll bet you could of gone to Cornell.

JOHN. Nancy please —

NANCY. And you, Dean, you got these super scores on your S.A.T.'s correct?

DEAN. 1370. *(Bobby returns from the bathroom, speeding.)*

BOBBY. 1370! Yeah!

NANCY. 1370, wow. Now just think, just think how much different, easier life might have been. What you could of done with those scores.

DEAN. Our mom died.

BOBBY. He wouldn't of done anything! Whew!

NANCY. But you understand what I'm saying?

DEAN. No.

BOBBY. No! No! No!

LIZ. You know this was my idea, Mrs. Roy —

MARY. *(To Bobby, private.)* Bobby, did you? How could you right now?

BOBBY. These people are driving me crazy.

MARY. Bobby.

BOBBY. What?

NANCY. You could of gone to Cornell.

DEAN. I didn't want to go to college.

BOBBY. He wouldn't of left me anyways!

NANCY. Of course you did, everyone wants to go to college.

LIZ. Oh no, not Dean, he wants to be a dad, work forty hours a week, drink beer and watch TV!

JOHN. This is enough, Nancy, it's getting out of control —

NANCY. I'm just trying to ask them, can they give Pollyanna all the opportunities a child should have?

DEAN. Polly's gonna do great on the S.A.T.'s because I'm her dad, and if she doesn't want to go to college, she won't, just like her dad.

LIZ. They don't give a shit about Pollyanna —

DEAN. Why are you doing this, Liz?

LIZ. Why? Because of the things you wanted to do, Dean —

DEAN. I know, I know —

LIZ. My god, if you can't stand and be honest you will lose everything —

DEAN. It's passed Liz, it's passed.

LIZ. But we, we — remember? *(Dean turns away from her.)* Fine! Die useless!

DEAN. I'm not gonna die useless! Why don't you take a look at your own life!

BOBBY. *(Exploding from the drugs and excitement in the room.)* That's right! Sock it 'em, Dean! See, he loves me, he didn't want to go, he wanted to stay with me after our mom died, he wanted to, right, Dean? Right?

DEAN. That's right.

BOBBY. Me and Polly and Liz and Mary, beautiful Mary, Mary who knows me better than anyone! We were making spaghetti, everything was fine!

LIZ. This isn't supposed to happen like this.

NANCY. Is he on drugs? He's on drugs. Isn't he? How can you, Mary? How can you let your beautiful, beautiful baby grow up in an environment with someone who is on drugs? How can you? Look, Mary —

LIZ. Oh god —

BOBBY. I've got such a headache, man.

NANCY. Do you want this around Pollyanna? Do you want this around her?

MARY. No.

NANCY. Well, then take a good look at your friend over there, take a good look —

DEAN. I think we'll go home and think about this.

JOHN. That's a good idea, it's a big decision.

NANCY. I sit across from these kids every day, these kids with nothing, and you know why? because their parents were nothing —

LIZ. Not nothing.

NANCY. And I think, why couldn't I be a mother? Huh? Why

them? All of them, and why not me?

JOHN. *(Coming towards her, tender.)* I know, Nancy, I know.

NANCY. So fuck you, John, fuck you. You think you can make the world a better place, they don't know what they want.

JOHN. God!

NANCY. Addiction is beyond your control, you told me that.

JOHN. This isn't about us!

NANCY. Yes it is, now it is. Isn't it, Liz? You told me to stay in the room, I wanted to wait in the car, you said: Stay, this has to do with you too. Didn't you? *(Liz shrugs.)*

JOHN. Listen to yourself, Nancy, c'mon, look at me —

NANCY. *(To John.)* Tell me how you would feel if you found out, in a year, let's say, that Pollyanna was dead, neglected, murdered accidentally in a crazed drug situation. It could be prevented. You could have prevented —

JOHN. I can't prevent anything —

NANCY. Think that, go ahead and think that along with everything else and you'll be back in the bars in no time.

JOHN. *(For himself, trying to hold it together.)* Acceptance, acceptance is the key to all my problems today.

NANCY. This is not an AA meeting!

JOHN. *(Huge, totally uncharacteristic for John.)* POLLYANNA IS NOT YOUR BABY! *(Quiet.)* Pollyanna is not going to save you, us. *(More quiet; Bobby holds his head.)*

BOBBY. Can we go home now, my stomach is like on fire. *(Dean goes to collect Mary, then turn to Liz to say good-bye; it's hard.)*

DEAN. Liz …

LIZ. Hey, you go for it.

MARY. Pollyanna will be okay, Mrs. Roy.

NANCY. *(Quiet.)* Really?

MARY. Bobby will leave.

DEAN. What?

MARY. He'll move away, far away. Dean will know it's right.

BOBBY. Mary?

MARY. It'll be the hardest for me, though, 'cause Bobby's been my best friend. We love each other so much. But he has to go away. If we want the baby, Bobby has to go away, and I'll get help, he'll go away, and I'll get help. Right, Dean?

BOBBY.   DEAN.
Mary?   Oh god, Mary —

MARY. Don't you think? Bobby? It's right? Right? You have to go away.

BOBBY. Where would I go?

MARY. Far away.

BOBBY. Dean?

DEAN. He's my only family.

MARY. Me and Polly, we're your family.

DEAN. He's my brother.

MARY. I love you, Bob, you know that, it's got nothing to do with you, it's about the baby, and well, the stuff, you know, the stuff. I look at Polly, Bob, and I see something good I finally did, and I want to keep that —

BOBBY. I'm good.

MARY. Oh I know that, Bob, it's not that, it's … you know what I'm trying to say, Dean?

DEAN. No, I don't, what?

MARY. When you hold her —

DEAN. I don't know, Mary — *(Mary goes to Dean, presses Pollyanna into his arms.)*

MARY. Look at her, you gotta feel this, you gotta want to keep her, this, this, beautiful, beautiful thing. *(Dean looks at Pollyanna in his arms, at Mary …)*

BOBBY. Dean?

DEAN. I'm sorry.

BOBBY. What, Dean?

DEAN. I want Polly, Bob.

BOBBY. You can't do that, you don't even know Polly.

DEAN. It doesn't mean I don't love you —

BOBBY. Yeah right, you couldn't love me and do this, no way —

MARY. Please, Bob, 'cause, would you stop?

BOBBY. No, no way, no, no, no fucking way, fuck you. Dean? Dean? You're not gonna make me leave, are you?

DEAN. I want her, Bob, I want her.

BOBBY. No, Dean.

DEAN. When we take the road trip we'll visit you.

BOBBY. Guys?

MARY. It's for the best, Bob, It'll be good. It'll be okay.

DEAN. I'm a dad now, Bobby.

LIZ. What is the big fucking deal with this stupid baby!?! *(She pleads with them.)* What? You just get thrown into the world, into life, hey kid, make a choice, it's wrong, make another one, it's right, step up to the plate, fight? Work? What? Have a baby? Go back to school? Is that the answer? You just keep trying and trying and trying? *(The baby cries. Dean nods. Liz listens to the baby, sees Dean holding her carefully. They stand there listening to the baby cry as the lights fade.)*

End of Play

PROPERTY LIST

Beer
Drug concoction on plate
Sneakers (JOHN, NANCY)
Polaroid camera (LIZ)
Hamburger meat (BOBBY)
Sony boom box (BOBBY)
Pot of boiling water (BOBBY)
Milk (BOBBY)
Glass (BOBBY)
Pan (BOBBY, NANCY, DEAN)
Oil (BOBBY)
Makings of dinner (NANCY)
Box of things (JOHN)
Roll of child's wallpaper (JOHN)
Photo (JOHN)
Dishes (DEAN)
Letter (LIZ)
Fried egg (NANCY)
Eggs (JOHN)
Bread (JOHN)
Jacket (DEAN)
Key hanging on a string (BOBBY)
Pots (DEAN, LIZ)
Package of spaghetti (DEAN, BOBBY)
Glass of water (NANCY)
Newspaper (JOHN)
S.A.T. scores (DEAN)
Baby wrapped in blankets (MARY)
White rock (drug) (BOBBY)
Pasta sauce (BOBBY)

SOUND EFFECTS

Heavy breathing and moaning
Baby crying

NEW PLAYS

★ **THE CIDER HOUSE RULES, PARTS 1 & 2 by Peter Parnell, adapted from the novel by John Irving.** Spanning eight decades of American life, this adaptation from the Irving novel tells the story of Dr. Wilbur Larch, founder of the St. Cloud's, Maine orphanage and hospital, and of the complex father-son relationship he develops with the young orphan Homer Wells. "…luxurious digressions, confident pacing…an enterprise of scope and vigor…" *–NY Times.* "…The fact that I can't wait to see Part 2 only begins to suggest just how good it is…" *–NY Daily News.* "…engrossing…an odyssey that has only one major shortcoming: It comes to an end." *–Seattle Times.* "…outstanding…captures the humor, the humility…of Irving's 588-page novel…" *–Seattle Post-Intelligencer.* [9M, 10W, doubling, flexible casting] PART 1 ISBN: 0-8222-1725-2 PART 2 ISBN: 0-8222-1726-0

★ **TEN UNKNOWNS by Jon Robin Baitz.** An iconoclastic American painter in his seventies has his life turned upside down by an art dealer and his ex-boyfriend. "…breadth and complexity…a sweet and delicate harmony rises from the four cast members…Mr. Baitz is without peer among his contemporaries in creating dialogue that spontaneously conveys a character's social context and moral limitations…" *–NY Times.* "…darkly funny, brilliantly desperate comedy…TEN UNKNOWNS vibrates with vital voices." *–NY Post.* [3M, 1W] ISBN: 0-8222-1826-7

★ **BOOK OF DAYS by Lanford Wilson.** A small-town actress playing St. Joan struggles to expose a murder. "…[Wilson's] best work since *Fifth of July*…An intriguing, prismatic and thoroughly engrossing depiction of contemporary small-town life with a murder mystery at its core…a splendid evening of theater…" *–Variety.* "…fascinating…a densely populated, unpredictable little world." *–St. Louis Post-Dispatch.* [6M, 5W] ISBN: 0-8222-1767-8

★ **THE SYRINGA TREE by Pamela Gien.** Winner of the 2001 Obie Award. A breathtakingly beautiful tale of growing up white in apartheid South Africa. "Instantly engaging, exotic, complex, deeply shocking…a thoroughly persuasive transport to a time and a place…stun[s] with the power of a gut punch…" *–NY Times.* "Astonishing…affecting …[with] a dramatic and heartbreaking conclusion…A deceptive sweet simplicity haunts THE SYRINGA TREE…" *–A.P.* [1W (or flexible cast)] ISBN: 0-8222-1792-9

★ **COYOTE ON A FENCE by Bruce Graham.** An emotionally riveting look at capital punishment. "The language is as precise as it is profane, provoking both troubling thought and the occasional cheerful laugh…will change you a little before it lets go of you." *–Cincinnati CityBeat.* "…excellent theater in every way…" *–Philadelphia City Paper.* [3M, 1W] ISBN: 0-8222-1738-4

★ **THE PLAY ABOUT THE BABY by Edward Albee.** Concerns a young couple who have just had a baby and the strange turn of events that transpire when they are visited by an older man and woman. "An invaluable self-portrait of sorts from one of the few genuinely great living American dramatists…rockets into that special corner of theater heaven where words shoot off like fireworks into dazzling patterns and hues." *–NY Times.* "An exhilarating, wicked…emotional terrorism." *–NY Newsday.* [2M, 2W] ISBN: 0-8222-1814-3

★ **FORCE CONTINUUM by Kia Corthron.** Tensions among black and white police officers and the neighborhoods they serve form the backdrop of this discomfiting look at life in the inner city. "The creator of this intense…new play is a singular voice among American playwrights…exceptionally eloquent…" *–NY Times.* "…a rich subject and a wise attitude." *–NY Post.* [6M, 2W, 1 boy] ISBN: 0-8222-1817-8

DRAMATISTS PLAY SERVICE, INC.
440 Park Avenue South, New York, NY 10016 212-683-8960 Fax 212-213-1539
postmaster@dramatists.com www.dramatists.com